Just the Opposite

Hard
Soft

Sharon Gordon

BENCHMARK BOOKS

MARSHALL CAVENDISH
NEW YORK

This apple is hard.

This apple is soft.

This hat is hard.

This hat is soft.

This egg is hard.

This egg is soft.

This ball is hard.

This ball is soft.

This candy is hard.

This candy is soft.

This chair is hard.

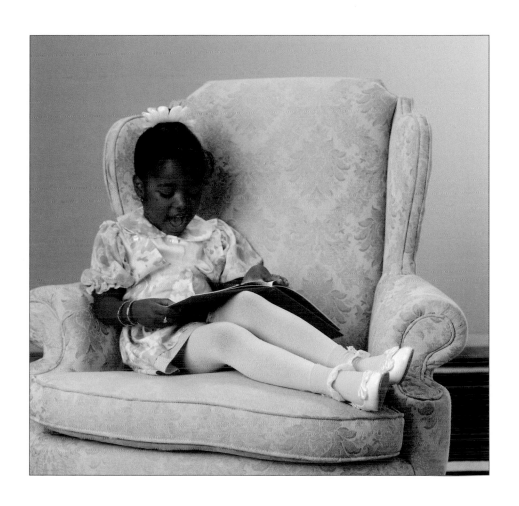

This chair is soft.

This cup is hard.

This cup is soft.

This doll is hard.

This doll is soft.

This ice cream is hard.

This ice cream is soft!

Words We Know

apple

ball

candy

chair

cup   doll   egg

hat   ice cream

Index

About the Author

Sharon Gordon has written many books for young children. She has also worked as an editor. Sharon and her husband Bruce have three children, Douglas, Katie, and Laura, and one spoiled pooch, Samantha. They live in Midland Park, New Jersey.

With thanks to Nanci Vargus, Ed.D.
and Beth Walker Gambro, reading consultants

Benchmark Books
Marshall Cavendish
99 White Plains Road
Tarrytown, New York 10591-9001
www.marshallcavendish.com

Library of Congress Cataloging-in-Publication Data

Gordon, Sharon.
Hard soft / by Sharon Gordon.
p. cm. — (Bookworms: Just the opposite)
Summary: Uses everyday examples, such as a baseball and a beach ball,
to demonstrate the contrast between hard and soft objects.
Includes index.
ISBN 0-7614-1571-8
1. Matter—Properties—Juvenile literature. 2. Touch—Juvenile
literature. 3. Polarity—Juvenile literature. 4. English
language—Synonyms and antonyms—Juvenile literature. [1. Hardness. 2.
English language—Synonyms and antonyms.] I. Title II. Series:
Gordon, Sharon. Bookworms: Just the opposite.

QC173.16.G67 2004
530.4'12—dc21
2003010081

Photo Research by Anne Burns Images

Cover Photos: *Corbis*: (top-Theresa Vargo), (bottom-Robert Holmes)
The photographs in this book are used with permission and through the courtesy of: *Corbis*: pp. 1 left, 16, 21 (top left) Rob Lewine; pp. 1 right, 17 Jose Luis Pelaez, Inc.; pp. 2, 20 (top left) Norbert Schaefer; pp. 4, 21 (top right) Jim Cummins; p. 5 Bill Miles; pp. 7, 13, 18, 21 (bottom left) Royalty Free; pp. 8, 20 (top right) Scott Wohrman; p. 9 Kim Robbie; p. 10 Theresa Vargo; pp. 11, 20 (bottom left) Robert Holmes; pp. 12, 20 (bottom right) Ariel Skelley; p. 14 Annie Griffiths; p. 15 Owen Franken; pp. 19, 21 (bottom right) James Leynse/SABA. *SWA Photo*: pp. 3, 6.

Series design by Becky Terhune

Printed in China
1 3 5 6 4 2

DEC   2007